Teamwork
MATH
Test Practice

GRADE
8

by Joyce Conway and Cindy T. Reiland

TABLE OF CONTENTS

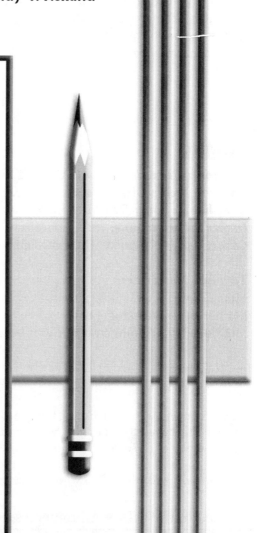

Carson-Dellosa Publishing Company, Inc.
Greensboro, North Carolina

Introduction

Teamwork Math Test Practice is designed to provide students with test-taking practice by introducing them to the format and content of the standardized tests they will encounter. This book does not replace effective teaching strategies, but rather it supplements the classroom teacher's existing curriculum and provides testing practice that will enable students to demonstrate what they have learned. Each practice test addresses the main math objectives and student expectations for eighth grade. The matrix on pages 3–5 conveniently references the standard and skill addressed in each math problem. Cross-curricular instructional strategies and engaging skill-based activities that have been correlated with standards are provided in *Teamwork Test Prep —Grade 8 Math* (CD-2241). A specific section on test-taking strategies is also included in the teacher resource book.

This book contains a variety of multiple-choice questions that are representative of most states' standards. There are four comprehensive tests that may be used as pretest/posttest assessment tools. Each test contains Part A and Part B sections that can be completed separately. At the end of each Part B, there is a question that requires a short written response. Students may answer those questions on the back of the test pages. If appropriate, allow students to use the Math Reference Chart when working with formulas. A grid and bubble answer sheet is included on page 47 to familiarize students with tracking. *Note: Remind students to cross out any row of bubbles that will not be used depending on the test they are taking.*

Credits

Authors: Joyce Conway and Cindy T. Reiland
Editors: Debra Olson Pressnall and Kelly Morris Huxmann
Graphic Layout: River Road Graphics
Inside Illustrations: Marty Bucella
Cover Design: Annette Hollister-Papp and Peggy Jackson

Teacher Reviewer:
Mike Lenzo
Mathematics Educator
Middle School Administrator, Twinsburg City Schools, Ohio

ISBN: 1-59441-143-3

Matrix/Objectives

Test Question Addressing Skill

Number Sense

Skills	Practice Test 1	2	3	4
Numeration and quantitative reasoning; compare and order positive and negative integers	13	4	2	4
Compare and order rational numbers in various forms including integers, percentages, and positive and negative fractions and decimals	1	35	51	4, 18
Represent numbers in scientific notation (positive and negative exponents)	16	7	23	10
Use order of operations and properties to simplify numerical expressions with integers, fractions, and decimals	44	8, 15	37	6, 15
Explain the meaning and effects of arithmetic operations with fractions, decimals, and integers	24	29	30	
Identify monomials and polynomials	8	6		12
Understand and use inverse relationships of addition and subtraction, multiplication, and division, and squaring and finding square roots to simplify computations and solve problems	30, 44	44	16	
Understand and use ratios and proportions to represent quantitative relationships	36	42, 46	35, 51	
Estimate the products and quotients of fractions and decimals and determine the reasonableness of the results	24	13	20	13
Demonstrate an understanding of absolute value	1, 11	5	7, 17, 36	4, 9, 18

Computation

Skills	Practice Test 1	2	3	4
Add, subtract, multiply, and divide positive and negative integers	27, 39, 40, 44	15	7, 11, 29	52
Add, subtract, multiply, and divide positive fractions and mixed numbers	37	50	11, 47	40
Simplify numeric expressions involving integers and use integers to solve real-life problems	41, 44	31	25	
Solve problems that involve fractions, decimals, and percentages	10, 31, 36	2, 13, 51	14, 20, 32	3
Convert between fractions, decimals, and percentages	3	17, 35	12, 20	16, 18
Use factors, multiples, prime factorization, and relatively prime numbers to solve problems	33	36	41	31, 33

Test Question Addressing Skill

Skills	Practice Test 1	Practice Test 2	Practice Test 3	Practice Test 4
Calculate simple and compound interest	28	9	28, 50	5
Calculate powers of integers and square roots of perfect square whole numbers	5	5, 10	17, 30, 37	44
Algebra				
Represent and analyze patterns, rules, functions with words, table, graphs, variables, and symbolic expressions	45	38	11	22
Solve linear equations with one and two variables	11, 32, 45	22, 37, 39	16, 38, 46	11, 20
Compare and contrast proportional and nonproportional relationships	36		21	50
Represent linear equations by plotting points on the coordinate plane		43	13	42
Represent inequalities on a number line or coordinate plane	6	24, 45	49	25
Explain how two forms of an algebraic expression can be equivalent or simplified	41	21	40	24, 43
Use formulas when solving problems	20, 21, 22, 46	1, 11	15, 46	8, 17, 28, 38
Find slope of linear functions	17	32		30
Analyze linear and nonlinear relationships to explain how a change in one variable results in the change of another		23		23
Identify x- and y-intercepts from a graph	2	18		21
Use models and numbers to solve one-step linear equations and inequalities in one variable	6	44	49	43
Carry out the four fundamental operations of simple algebraic expressions using monomials and polynomials	38	21, 48	29	19
Geometry				
Describe, classify, and understand relationships among types of two and three-dimensional objects using their defining properties (including triangles, quadrilaterals, pentagons, circles, pyramids, cones, prisms, and cylinders)	43	3, 41	3, 9	39
Analyze properties of plane geometric figures and geometric relationships (determine missing angle measurements using the sum of interior angles of polygons)	32	20, 22, 40	26, 42	20
Find geometric properties of a figure in a plane and confirm them by using properties of parallel and perpendicular lines	48	47	10	41
Clarify the concepts and properties of similarity and congruency of triangles and prove them	35	30, 40	24, 43	7, 34
Use pictures or models to demonstrate the Pythagorean Theorem	30	25	48	27, 37
Understand the meaning of congruency and conditions for congruent triangles	7	34	24, 39	48

Test Question Addressing Skill

Skills	Practice Test 1	2	3	4
Draw representations of three-dimensional geometric objects from different views	9	3	36	
Perform translations, reflections, rotations, and dilations of two-dimensional figures using a variety of methods	26	49	27	49, 51
Determine volume of cones, prisms, pyramids, cylinders, and spheres	21, 22, 34, 43	16, 33	5, 15	17, 47
Determine surface area of cylinders, prisms, and pyramids; determine area of two-dimensional objects	20, 21, 43	27, 31	3, 19, 34	35, 38
Estimate a measurement to a greater degree of precision that the tool provides	46	26	45	
Solve problems involving proportional relationships and scale factors	25, 29	26	8, 35	28, 47
Connect models to formulas for volume of prisms, cylinders, pyramids, and cones	47	16	6	14
Use proportional relationships in similar shapes to find missing measurements	14	40	43	34
Describe the resulting effect on perimeter and area when dimensions of a shape are changed proportionally	18	46		2
Describe the resulting effect on volume when dimensions of a solid are changed proportionally	34	33	5	28, 47
Convert measurements between the customary and metric systems	46	1, 11		8, 26
Convert measurements within the same measurement system	39	14		26
Draw conclusions and make predictions by analyzing trends in scatter plots; interpret box-and-whisker plots	4, 23		1	
Construct and interpret circle graphs, line graphs, and bar graphs	10, 12, 23			36, 46
Analyze how decisions about graphing affect the graphical representation			44	46
Evaluate methods of sampling to determine validity of an inference made from a set of data; interpret data collected	49	48	4, 51	
Determine and compare the mean, median, and mode of a set of data; determine quartiles of box-and-whiskers plots	23	28	32	29
Determine probability of an event comprised of no more than 2 independent events	42	12, 19	22	1
Compare the results of theoretical probability and experimental probability	15		33	
Make predictions based on theoretical probabilities	19	19	31	32

Measurements

Data Analysis and Probability

Math Reference Chart

Key

l = length	P = perimeter	A = area
w = width	SA = surface area	V = volume
s = length of a side	d = diameter	B = area of the base of a solid
b = base	r = radius	
h = height	C = circumference	$\pi \approx 3.14$ or $\frac{22}{7}$

The sum of the interior angles of a polygon is equal to $180(n-2)$,
where n is the number of sides in the polygon.

Perimeter

square $\quad P = 4s$
rectangle $\quad P = 2(l + w)$

Circumference

circle $\quad C = 2\pi r$ or πd

Pythagorean Theorem

$a^2 + b^2 = c^2$

Area

□	square	$A = s^2$
▭	rectangle	$A = lw$ or bh
△	triangle	$A = \frac{1}{2}bh$ or $\frac{bh}{2}$
⬠	trapezoid	$A = \frac{1}{2}(b_1 + b_2)h$ or $\frac{(b_1 + b_2)h}{2}$
▱	parallelogram	$A = bh$
○	circle	$A = \pi r^2$

Surface Area

⬛	cube	$SA = 6s^2$
▭	rectangular solid	$SA = 2(lw) + 2(hw) + 2(lh)$
⬭	cylinder (total)	$SA = 2\pi rh + 2\pi r^2$
⊖	sphere	$SA = 4\pi r^2$

Volume

▭	rectangular solid	$V = lwh$
▯	prism	$V = Bh$
⬭	cylinder	$V = \pi r^2 h$
△	pyramid	$V = \frac{1}{3}Bh$
⊖	sphere	$V = \frac{4}{3}\pi r^3$

Practice Math Test   **Part A**

Directions: Find the correct answer.

1 Which set shows the given numbers ordered from least to greatest?

$\frac{3}{8}$ **38%**   **0.0038**   **|-3.8|**

  Ⓐ 38% $\frac{3}{8}$ 0.0038 |-3.8|

  Ⓑ |-3.8| $\frac{3}{8}$ 0.0038   38%

  Ⓒ 0.0038 $\frac{3}{8}$ 38% |-3.8|

  Ⓓ 0.0038 |-3.8| 38% $\frac{3}{8}$

2 Choose the graph that has *x*-intercept (-3, 0) and *y*-intercept (0, 3).

  Ⓕ
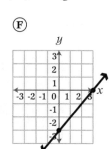

  Ⓖ
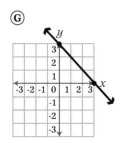

  Ⓗ
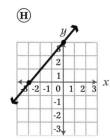

  Ⓙ
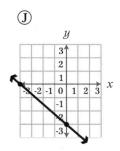

3 Which numbers are equivalent to **1.5**?

  Ⓐ 15%, $\frac{5}{2}$, |1.5|

  Ⓑ 1.5%, $\frac{6}{4}$, |1.5|

  Ⓒ 150%, $\frac{5}{2}$, |-1.5|

  Ⓓ 150%, $\frac{6}{4}$, |-1.5|

4 The graph below shows the distance from Miguel's home to the video store and the time it took him to get there.

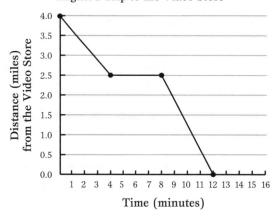

Miguel's Trip to the Video Store

Which statement about Miguel's trip is NOT true?

  Ⓕ The video store is 4 miles from Miguel's house.

  Ⓖ After Miguel had traveled for 4 minutes, he was $2\frac{1}{2}$ miles from the video store.

  Ⓗ Miguel traveled the greatest distance in the span of 4 to 8 minutes.

  Ⓙ Miguel took 12 minutes to reach the video store.

5 Estimate: $\sqrt{27}$ is between _____.

  Ⓐ 13 and 14

  Ⓑ 5 and 6

  Ⓒ 6 and 7

  Ⓓ 12 and 13

GO ON

Practice Math Test 1 (continued)

6 Which graph represents the solution for the following inequality?

$$3x - 6 \leq 12$$

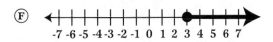

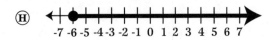

7 $\triangle ABC$ is congruent to $\triangle DEF$. What is the measure of $\angle F$?

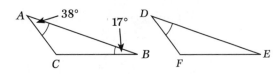

ⓐ 55°

ⓑ 110°

ⓒ 125°

ⓓ 135°

8 Which expression is NOT a polynomial?

Ⓕ $-7x + 20$

Ⓖ $\frac{1}{2}x - 19$

Ⓗ $5x - 1$

Ⓙ $\frac{3}{x} - 5$

9 Which figure can be folded to form a cube?

ⓐ

ⓑ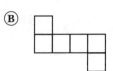

ⓒ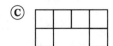

ⓓ

10 Four hundred eighth-grade students were surveyed about their eye color. The results are shown in the graph.

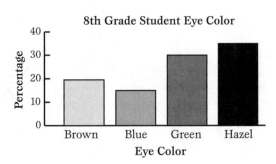

According to the data, approximately how many students had green eyes?

Ⓕ 140 students

Ⓖ 120 students

Ⓗ 80 students

Ⓙ 30 students

11 Find $| x - 5 |$ when $x = -2$.

ⓐ -3

ⓑ 7

ⓒ -7

ⓓ 3

GO ON

12 The bar graph shows the number of pets a group of children had. Match the circle graph that best represents the data shown in the bar graph.

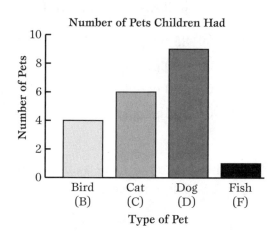

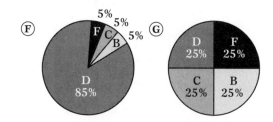

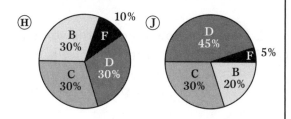

13 Which expression is TRUE?

Ⓐ -16 > -15

Ⓑ -16 < -20

Ⓒ -16 > 1

Ⓓ -16 < -3

14 The polygons below are similar. Find the length of **C** if **B = 24 meters**.

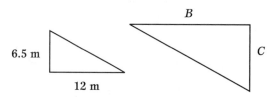

Ⓕ 18.5 meters

Ⓖ 39 meters

Ⓗ 13 meters

Ⓙ 48 meters

15 Sanchu tossed a fair coin 100 times. She was surprised when 30 of the tosses showed heads. Which statement best explains why she was surprised?

Ⓐ She expected fewer than 30 of the tosses to show heads.

Ⓑ She expected almost all of the tosses to come up heads.

Ⓒ She expected many more of the tosses to be tails.

Ⓓ She expected closer to 50 of the tosses to be heads.

16 In 1997, the population of China was approximately 1,240,000,000. What is this population written in scientific notation?

Ⓕ 1.24×10^9

Ⓖ 124×10^7

Ⓗ 1.24×10^8

Ⓙ 12.4×10^8

GO ON ➡

Practice Math Test 1 (continued)

17 What is the slope of the line?

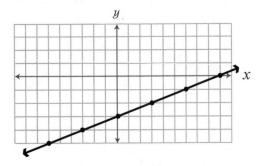

   Ⓐ 3

   Ⓑ $\frac{1}{3}$

   Ⓒ $-\frac{1}{3}$

   Ⓓ -3

18 Look at the diagram. The Gianoli family has a fence surrounding a space in their backyard. The family wants to double the width and length of the space. How will the perimeter and area change?

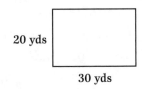

20 yds

30 yds

   Ⓕ The perimeter will double.
      The area will be 4 times as large.

   Ⓖ The perimeter will double.
      The area will remain the same.

   Ⓗ The perimeter will stay the
      same. The area will double.

   Ⓙ The perimeter will be 4 times
      as large. The area will double.

19 The probability that a person can curl his or her tongue is 0.85. If you survey 200 people about whether they can curl their tongues, approximately how many people will say they can do this?

   Ⓐ 85 people

   Ⓑ 130 people

   Ⓒ 170 people

   Ⓓ 185 people

20 What is the radius of a circle if its area is 12.56 square meters?

Use: $A = \pi r^2$

$\pi = 3.14$

   Ⓕ 9.46 meters

   Ⓖ 6.32 meters

   Ⓗ 4 meters

   Ⓙ 2 meters

21 About how much is the volume of a tennis ball if its diameter is 2.5 inches?

Use: $V = \frac{4}{3}\pi r^3$

   Ⓐ 4.59 in.³

   Ⓑ 6.54 in.³

   Ⓒ 8.18 in.³

   Ⓓ 9.42 in.³

GO ON

22 Find the volume for the cylinder below.
Use: **V = Bh**

π = **3.14**

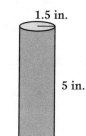

1.5 in.

5 in.

Ⓕ 35.325 in.³

Ⓖ 37.5 in.³

Ⓗ 43.55 in.³

Ⓙ 47.1 in.³

23 The stem-and-leaf plot shows the average daily temperature in degrees Fahrenheit for Santiago, Chile, for the first 11 days in March. Draw a box-and-whisker plot for the data to answer the question.

Stem	Leaf
9	4 6 6 6 8
10	1 1 1 1 3 5

Key: 10 | 5 = 105°F

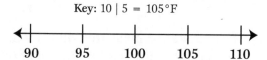

90   95   100   105   110

Which statement is TRUE according to the data?

Ⓐ The median is 100°F.

Ⓑ Most of the temperatures are higher than the median.

Ⓒ The second quartile is 101°F.

Ⓓ There is no mode.

24 Choose the statement that best describes the product of the expression.

$$\frac{3}{4} \times 0.2$$

Ⓕ The product will be twice as large as $\frac{3}{4}$ because it is being multiplied by 2.

Ⓖ The product will be less than 0.2 because it is being multiplied by $\frac{3}{4}$, which is less than 1.

Ⓗ The product will be greater than $\frac{3}{4}$ because when you multiply the product always gets larger.

Ⓙ The product will be between $\frac{3}{4}$ and 0.2

25 A scale drawing of a flagpole is shown below. Next to the scale drawing is part of a ruler.

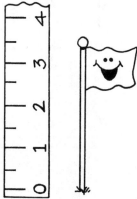

If the scale used is 1 inch = 9 feet, about how tall is the actual flagpole?

Ⓐ 27 feet

Ⓑ 31.5 feet

Ⓒ 33.5 feet

Ⓓ 36 feet

for Part A

Practice Math Test 1 (continued)

26 Which graph would result if rectangle *ABCD* is reflected across the *x*-axis and translated 5 units to the left?

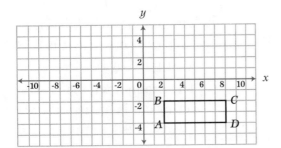

(F)

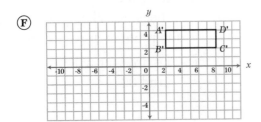

(G)

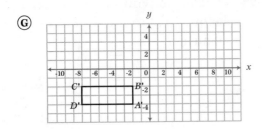

(H)

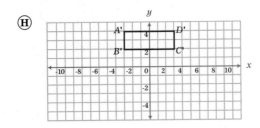

(J)

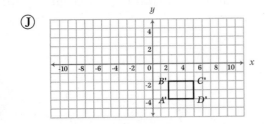

27 Which answer choice contains solutions to the given problems in the order they are written?

-15×3 $-15 \div -3$ $-15 + 3$ $-15 - 3$

   Ⓐ -45, 5, -12, -18

   Ⓑ 45, -5, 12, -12

   Ⓒ -45, -5, -12, 18

   Ⓓ 45, 5, -12, 12

28 Michelle deposited $800 into an account that earned 5% interest compounded every 6 months. How much did Michelle have in the account after 1 year?

   Ⓕ $805

   Ⓖ $840

   Ⓗ $880

   Ⓙ $882

29 If the distance measured on the map between 2 cities is 3.38 inches, about how many miles does that represent?

Use the scale: **1 inch = 12.5 miles**.

   Ⓐ 48.5 miles

   Ⓑ 42.25 miles

   Ⓒ 40.75 miles

   Ⓓ 36.25 miles

GO ON

30 Brianna has a garden that measures 20 feet by 20 feet. She wants to fence off a triangular-shaped piece of the garden as shown below.

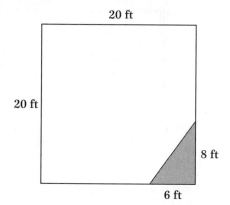

What is the perimeter of the triangular piece?

Ⓕ 14 feet

Ⓖ 19 feet

Ⓗ 24 feet

Ⓙ 80 feet

31 Due to an increase in gasoline prices, the cost of a round-trip bus ticket from Ohio to Florida is now 21% more than its original cost. If the original cost was $189, what is the new cost for the round-trip ticket?

Ⓐ $585.90

Ⓑ $228.69

Ⓒ $210.50

Ⓓ $149.31

32 Find the measure of each angle in the triangle shown below.

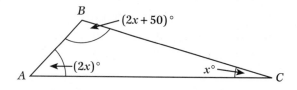

Ⓕ $\angle A = 60°$, $\angle B = 90°$, $\angle C = 30°$

Ⓖ $\angle A = 52°$, $\angle B = 102°$, $\angle C = 26°$

Ⓗ $\angle A = 92°$, $\angle B = 142°$, $\angle C = 46°$

Ⓙ $\angle A = 44°$, $\angle B = 104°$, $\angle C = 22°$

33 Which set of numbers is best described by ALL of these statements?

- Every even number is a multiple of 4.
- There are 2 prime numbers.
- Fifty percent of the numbers in the set are positive.

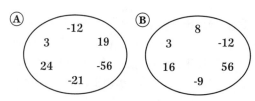

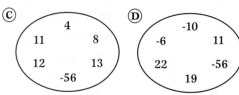

Practice Math Test 1 (continued)

34 A company makes boxes in 2 different sizes. One box is 3 inches by 3 inches by 2 inches. The other box is twice as large, or 6 inches by 6 inches by 4 inches. Which statement about the volumes of the boxes is TRUE?

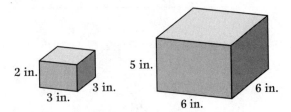

2 in. 3 in. 3 in.   5 in. 6 in. 6 in.

- Ⓕ The volumes of the boxes are equal.
- Ⓖ The volume of the larger box is twice the volume of the smaller box.
- Ⓗ The volume of the larger box is 3 times the volume of the smaller box.
- Ⓙ The volume of the larger box is 8 times the volume of the smaller box.

35 Rodney makes a drawing of a triangle and wants to make a similar triangle that is smaller. What must the triangles have in common to be similar?

- Ⓐ corresponding angles that are congruent
- Ⓑ equal altitudes
- Ⓒ equal areas
- Ⓓ corresponding sides that are congruent

36 The manufacturer of M&M's® reports the following percentages used when making plain M&M's.

Color	Percentages
blue	10%
brown	30%
green	10%
orange	10%
red	20%
yellow	20%

Maria bought a bag of M&M's® that had 55 pieces in it. Which proportion could be used to predict the number of red candies in the bag?

- Ⓕ $\frac{20}{100} = \frac{x}{55}$
- Ⓖ $\frac{20}{100} = \frac{55}{x}$
- Ⓗ $\frac{20}{55} = \frac{x}{55}$
- Ⓙ $\frac{10}{100} = \frac{x}{55}$

37 Add: $\frac{2}{3} + \frac{1}{2} + \frac{2}{5} + \frac{1}{10} =$

- Ⓐ $1\frac{1}{2}$
- Ⓑ $1\frac{1}{10}$
- Ⓒ $1\frac{2}{5}$
- Ⓓ $1\frac{2}{3}$

GO ON

Practice Math Test 1 (continued)

38 Simplify the expression:

$$3(x - 3) - 2(5x + 1)$$

- (F) $-7x - 2$
- (G) $13x - 8$
- (H) $8x - 7$
- (J) $-7x - 11$

39 A bow-making machine uses 18 inches of ribbon for each bow. How many bows can be made from 9.25 feet of ribbon?

- (A) 6 bows
- (B) 5 bows
- (C) 4 bows
- (D) 3 bows

40 Think about the temperatures below. Which answer shows an 11° increase?

- (F) 20° to 32°
- (G) -1° to 12°
- (H) -2° to 9°
- (J) -5° to 11°

41 Which expression can be simplified to **$5x - 12$**?

- (A) $3x + 2(x + 6)$
- (B) $4(x - 12) + x$
- (C) $3(2x - 4) - x$
- (D) $2x + 3(x - 9)$

42 A vending machine has 5 different kinds of candy bars, 3 kinds of chips, 4 kinds of gum, and 3 kinds of crackers. All items cost the same amount of money. Ramon deposits enough money to buy 1 item, then presses a selection button without looking. What is the probability that he selected a candy bar or gum?

- (F) $\frac{4}{5}$
- (G) $\frac{4}{13}$
- (H) $\frac{3}{5}$
- (J) $\frac{7}{15}$

43 Which statement is NOT true for the prism shown?

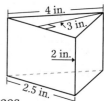

- (A) The solid has 5 faces. Two of them are triangles.
- (B) The volume of the prism is 9.5 in³.
- (C) The solid has 6 vertices and 9 edges.
- (D) The surface area of the prism is 28.5 in².

44 Simplify the expression:

$$-13 + 6 \div 2 \times 3 + \sqrt{49}$$

- (F) 3
- (G) -10.5
- (H) $-\frac{7}{3}$
- (J) -11

GO ON

45 The table shows values for x and y. Which equation represents the data?

Ⓐ $y = x - 1$

Ⓑ $y = x^2 - 1$

Ⓒ $y = 5x + 5$

Ⓓ $y = 3x^2 - 4$

x	y
1	0
2	3
3	8
4	15
5	24
6	35

46 Look at the thermometer. If the air temperature drops 5°F, what will the new reading be in degree Celsius?

Use: $C = \frac{5}{9}(F - 32)$.

Ⓕ 18°C

Ⓖ 20°C

Ⓗ 45°C

Ⓙ 65°C

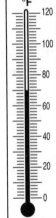

47 The formula for finding the volume of a cone is $V = \frac{1}{3}\pi r^2 h$. Select the answer closest to the volume of the cone pictured. Use: $\pi = 3.14$.

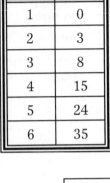

6 m

4 m

Ⓐ 4 m³

Ⓑ 12.56 m³

Ⓒ 25.12 m³

Ⓓ 37.68 m³

48 Which polygon is NOT a rectangle?

Ⓕ

4 in.   8 in.   8 in.   4 in.

Ⓖ

88°   92°

Ⓗ

6 in.

6 in.

90°

Ⓙ

49 Remington School wants to decide what after-school activities should be offered to the seventh and eighth graders. The school has a very large student population. The decision has been made to sample the student body and conduct a survey to find out the activities students are most interested in attending. Describe a sampling method that would best represent all seventh- and eighth-grade students.

Practice Math Test   **Part A**

Directions: Find the correct answer.

1 Tawana has been chosen to run the 100-meter dash for her track team. If this distance were measured in feet (f), about how far would she run?

Use: $f = m \cdot 3.28$

Ⓐ 33 feet

Ⓑ 175 feet

Ⓒ 330 feet

Ⓓ 400 feet

2 Craig, James, and Marty decide to split the cost of a super-sized pizza. The pizza costs $16.85. Craig pays $\frac{3}{7}$ of the cost, and James pays 32% of the cost. How much does Marty pay?

Ⓕ $7.22

Ⓖ $5.62

Ⓗ $5.40

Ⓙ $4.24

3 Look at the diagrams. Which figure can be folded into a rectangular prism?

Ⓐ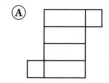

Ⓑ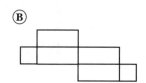

Ⓒ

Ⓓ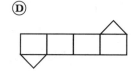

4 Arrange the given numbers in order from least to greatest value.

6   0   -15   -12   4   -1

Ⓕ 6, 4, 0, -1, -12, -15

Ⓖ -1, 0, 4, -12, -15, 6

Ⓗ 0, -1, 4, 6, -12, -15

Ⓙ -15, -12, -1, 0, 4, 6

5 Which choice shows the greatest value?

Ⓐ $|6|$

Ⓑ $\sqrt{49}$

Ⓒ $|-10|$

Ⓓ 9.573

6 A polynomial has _____ terms.

Ⓕ 2 or more

Ⓖ 1 or more

Ⓗ less than 1

Ⓙ exactly 4

7 The average distance from Earth to the Sun is 92,955,800 miles. Express this number in scientific notation.

Ⓐ 929.558×10^5

Ⓑ 92.9558×10^6

Ⓒ 92955.8×10^3

Ⓓ 9.29558×10^7

GO ON ➡

Part A

Practice Math Test 2 (continued)

8 Simplify: **-10(1 – 9) ÷ (-20) + 0.5(6)**

    Ⓕ -1

    Ⓖ 7

    Ⓗ -7

    Ⓙ 26

9 Lucas borrowed $7,500 from his mom to buy a car. He agreed to pay her simple interest of 4.5% and to pay off the debt in 12 months. How much will he pay for the loan?

    Ⓐ $10,875.00

    Ⓑ $7,837.50

    Ⓒ $7,750.00

    Ⓓ $337.50

10 Which expression has the greatest value?

    Ⓕ 3^3

    Ⓖ $\sqrt{81}$

    Ⓗ $\sqrt{16}$

    Ⓙ 4^2

11 If the air temperature is 98°F, what is the reading in degree Celsius?

    Use: $C = \frac{5}{9}(F - 32)$

    Ⓐ 208.4°C

    Ⓑ 118.8°C

    Ⓒ 66°C

    Ⓓ 36.7°C

12 Akiko reaches into a bowl and grabs 5 red, 4 green, 2 blue, 3 yellow, and 2 orange jelly beans. If she eats 1 candy without looking at it, what is the probability of eating a red or a yellow jelly bean?

    Ⓕ $\frac{7}{16}$

    Ⓖ $\frac{5}{16}$

    Ⓗ $\frac{1}{8}$

    Ⓙ $\frac{1}{2}$

13 Mrs. Baczynski walks into Squirrelly's Nut Shop and buys $1\frac{1}{2}$ pounds of peanuts, $\frac{3}{4}$ pound of cashews, and $1\frac{2}{3}$ pounds of walnuts. If she pays for her purchases with a 20-dollar bill, how many bags of popcorn could she buy with the change?

Squirrelly's Nut Shop

Cashews $6.60/lb

Peanuts $3.50/lb

Walnuts..................$4.75/lb

Popcorn..............$0.60/bag

    Ⓐ 0 bags of popcorn

    Ⓑ 1 bag of popcorn

    Ⓒ 2 bags of popcorn

    Ⓓ 3 bags of popcorn

Name: _____   Date: _____

14 A kilometer is _____ millimeters.

- (F) 100
- (G) 1,000
- (H) 10,000
- (J) 1,000,000

15 Solve the equation for n.

$$3[-4 \cdot (-3)] \div (-8 + 2) = n$$

- (A) $n = -6$
- (B) $n = 6$
- (C) $n = -8$
- (D) $n = 8$

16 To find the volume of the figure below, multiply the area of its base by its height. Which equation would you use to calculate its volume?

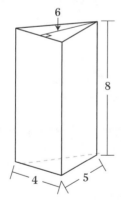

- (F) $V = 6 \cdot 4 \cdot 8$
- (G) $V = \frac{1}{2} \cdot 6 \cdot 4 \cdot 8$
- (H) $V = 4 \cdot 8 \cdot 5$
- (J) $V = \frac{1}{2} \cdot 4 \cdot 6 \cdot 5$

17 Which choice shows **0.656** written as a fraction?

- (A) $\frac{656}{100}$
- (B) $65 \frac{6}{100}$
- (C) $\frac{65}{100}$
- (D) $\frac{82}{125}$

18 On the graph, the x-intercept and the y-intercept are shown by which coordinates?

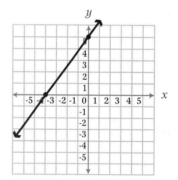

- (F) x-intercept $(0, -4)$
  y-intercept $(5, 0)$
- (G) x-intercept $(5, 0)$
  y-intercept $(-4, 0)$
- (H) x-intercept $(-4, 0)$
  y-intercept $(0, 5)$
- (J) x-intercept $(-4, 0)$
  y-intercept $(5, 0)$

GO ON

Practice Math Test 2 (continued)

19 If Olivia spins this spinner 100 times, how many times would you expect the pointer to land on an even number based on *theoretical probability*?

- Ⓐ 40 times
- Ⓑ 50 times
- Ⓒ 60 times
- Ⓓ 75 times

20 Which of the following angles is NOT an obtuse angle?

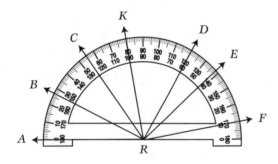

- Ⓕ ∠*ARD*
- Ⓖ ∠*BRE*
- Ⓗ ∠*FRK*
- Ⓙ ∠*DRB*

21 Simplify the expression:

$$3(x + 4) - (2x - 6)$$

- Ⓐ $5x + 6$
- Ⓑ $5x + 10$
- Ⓒ $x + 10$
- Ⓓ $x + 18$

22 What is the measure of ∠*ADC* in this quadrilateral?

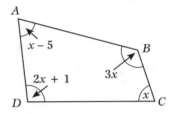

- Ⓕ 156°
- Ⓖ 105°
- Ⓗ 52°
- Ⓙ 47°

23 Think about the equation: $y^2 = x$. If y is divided in half, what happens to the value of x?

- Ⓐ The value of x is doubled.
- Ⓑ It is divided in half.
- Ⓒ The value of x is divided by 4.
- Ⓓ It stays the same.

24 The number line shows the solution for which inequality?

- Ⓕ $4x + 2 \leq 14$
- Ⓖ $2x - 1 < 3$
- Ⓗ $3x - 1 \leq 8$
- Ⓙ $x + 3 \leq 3$

for Part A

25 Using the Pythagorean Theorem, which equation can be used to find the measure of side c?

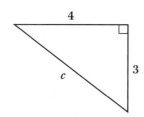

- Ⓐ $3^2 + c^2 = 4^2$
- Ⓑ $4^2 + c^2 = 3^2$
- Ⓒ $3 + 4 = c$
- Ⓓ $3^2 + 4^2 = c^2$

26 On a map drawn to scale, 5 centimeters equals 300 kilometers. How long would a line segment be that represents 450 kilometers?

- Ⓕ $2\frac{1}{2}$ centimeters
- Ⓖ $7\frac{1}{2}$ centimeters
- Ⓗ 10 centimeters
- Ⓙ 30 centimeters

27 Rico has a wooden cubic box for his sports gear. Each side of the box measures 3 feet. How many square feet of wood did he use to make his box?

- Ⓐ 8 ft^2
- Ⓑ 27 ft^2
- Ⓒ 48 ft^2
- Ⓓ 54 ft^2

28 Look at the table.

Average Days of Rain or
Snow for Lake Geneva

Month	Number of Days	Month	Number of Days
Jan.	13	July	13
Feb.	10	Aug.	10
Mar.	11	Sept.	8
April	11	Oct.	7
May	11	Nov.	8
June	9	Dec.	9

What are the mean, median, and mode for this set of data?

- Ⓕ mean 13, median 9, mode 7
- Ⓖ mean 10, median 10, mode 11
- Ⓗ mean 10, median 11, mode 10
- Ⓙ mean 9, median 11, mode 8

29 Which statement is NOT true?

- Ⓐ Multiplying a number by 2 is the same as dividing it by $\frac{1}{2}$.
- Ⓑ Adding 40% of a number to itself is the same as multiplying the number by $1\frac{2}{5}$.
- Ⓒ Dividing a number by 30% will result in a smaller number.
- Ⓓ Subtracting 30% of a number from itself is the same as multiplying the number by $\frac{7}{10}$.

GO ON

30 Quadrilateral *ABCD* is similar to *EFGH*. What is the measure of $\overline{FG}$?

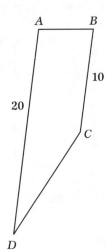 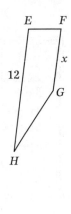

(F) 12   (G) 8

(H) 6   (J) 5

31 Carl will be planting an odd-shaped plot of land on his farm as shown in the diagram. How many square feet of land will be seeded?

Round to nearest whole number.
Use: π = **3.14**.

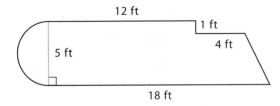

(A) 164 ft²

(B) 101 ft²

(C) 90 ft²

(D) 40 ft²

32 Which slope best describes the line?

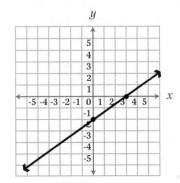

(F) $\frac{2}{3}$

(G) $\frac{3}{2}$

(H) $-\frac{2}{3}$

(J) $-\frac{3}{2}$

33 The volume of the cube shown below is 8 cubic centimeters. If each side of the cube is doubled in size, what will happen to its volume?

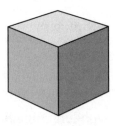

(A) The volume will be doubled.

(B) The volume will increase 3 times.

(C) The volume will increase 4 times.

(D) The volume will increase 8 times.

GO ON

34 If $\triangle RST \cong \triangle ABC$, side $\overline{BC}$ will be congruent to which corresponding side of $\triangle RST$?

 Ⓕ $\overline{RS}$

 Ⓖ $\overline{ST}$

 Ⓗ $\overline{RT}$

 Ⓙ $\overline{TR}$

35 Which answer shows the given values in order from greatest to least?

$\frac{2}{3}$ 0.075   37% |-1.075|

 Ⓐ $\frac{2}{3}$ |-1.075| 0.075   37%

 Ⓑ |-1.075| 0.075   37% $\frac{2}{3}$

 Ⓒ |-1.075| $\frac{2}{3}$ 37%   0.075

 Ⓓ 0.075 $\frac{2}{3}$ 37% |-1.075|

36 In Mrs. Reiland's classroom, every third student receives a blue folder, every fifth student gets a green notebook, and every other student is given a red pen. What is the position of the first child to receive all three items?

 Ⓕ seat 15

 Ⓖ seat 20

 Ⓗ seat 27

 Ⓙ seat 30

37 Solve to find the value of n:

$$\tfrac{1}{2}(n + 6) = 2(n - 3)$$

 Ⓐ $n = 5$

 Ⓑ $n = 6$

 Ⓒ $n = 7$

 Ⓓ $n = 8$

38 Choose the correct algebraic equation for the following expression:

Two times the difference of a number and six is less than or equal to the sum of three times the number and seven.

 Ⓕ $2(6 - n) \geq 3(n + 7)$

 Ⓖ $2(n - 6) < n + 7$

 Ⓗ $2(n - 6) \leq 3n + 7$

 Ⓙ $2(n - 6) = 3(n + 7)$

39 Solve this system of equations:

$$2y + 1 = 7$$
$$3x + 2y = 21$$

 Ⓐ $x = 2, y = 3$

 Ⓑ $x = 5, y = 3$

 Ⓒ $x = 0, y = 10\tfrac{1}{2}$

 Ⓓ $x = 3, y = 5$

GO ON ⟹

Practice Math Test 2 (continued)

40 $\triangle RMS$ is similar to $\triangle TNB$. Find the length of $\overline{NT}$. Round the number to the nearest hundredth.

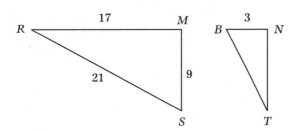

     Ⓕ 4.93

     Ⓖ 5.36

     Ⓗ 5.67

     Ⓙ 5.70

41 Which figure will NOT have all angles congruent?

     Ⓐ equilateral triangle

     Ⓑ square

     Ⓒ regular hexagon

     Ⓓ obtuse triangle

42 Out of 200 boys at Randolph School, 3 out of 5 like to play trench ball. About how many boys do NOT enjoy playing this game?

     Ⓕ 60 boys

     Ⓖ 80 boys

     Ⓗ 100 boys

     Ⓙ 120 boys

43 If you were to plot the following points, which line contains the ordered pairs?

x	y
0	3
-3	0
-2	1

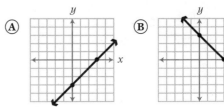

44 Which expression has the greatest value?

     Ⓕ $\sqrt{144} + 3(-14)$

     Ⓖ $62 - \frac{1}{2}(-8)$

     Ⓗ $7^2 - \sqrt{121}$

     Ⓙ $|-16| + 3(12 - 7)$

GO ON

45 Which number line shows the solution to this inequality?

$$6x - 4 \geq 2x + 8$$

Ⓐ

Ⓑ

Ⓒ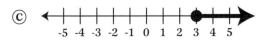

Ⓓ

46 Toni wants to set up a new pen for her pet goat. If she triples the size of the pen, what will be the effect on its perimeter and area?

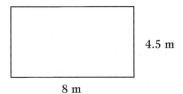

4.5 m

8 m

Ⓕ The area will double in size; the perimeter will triple in size.

Ⓖ Both the perimeter and the area will triple in size.

Ⓗ The perimeter will triple in size; the area will increase 9 times.

Ⓙ The perimeter will triple in size; the area will increase 6 times.

47 Line *l* is parallel to line *m*, and line *r* is parallel to line *t*. Using this information, what do you know about figure *ABCD*?

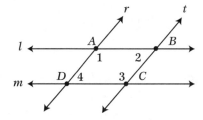

Ⓐ ∠1 and ∠3 are congruent.

Ⓑ ∠1 and ∠2 are congruent.

Ⓒ ∠1, ∠2, ∠3, and ∠4 are all congruent.

Ⓓ ∠1 + ∠3 must equal 180°.

48 Sakari attends a large high school that plans to change its mascot. She is responsible for making a list of the choices on which the students will vote. How should she collect the information for her survey question?

Ⓕ Ask every student so that everyone has a voice.

Ⓖ Let the teachers choose because they are older and have better ideas.

Ⓗ Let the senior-class members choose because it is their last year in high school.

Ⓙ Ask the student council for choices since it represents all of the students.

GO ON ▷

Practice Math Test 2 (continued)

49 Which expression simplifies to **$4x - 8$**?

    Ⓐ $12(x + 1) - 6(x - 1)$

    Ⓑ $8x + 5(-x + 3)$

    Ⓒ $12(2 - x) + 8(2x - 4)$

    Ⓓ $10(x + 2) - 4(x + 3) - 5$

50 Look at the graph. Processes have been used to move the house from Quadrant I to Quadrant IV. Which answer choice lists the order of transformations correctly?

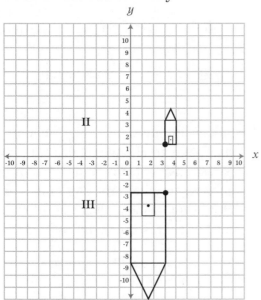

1) reflection
2) rotation—180° around the origin
3) dilation
4) translation—four units to the right

    Ⓕ   processes 4, 1, and 3

    Ⓖ   processes 2, 4, and 3

    Ⓗ   processes 2, 3, and 1

    Ⓙ   processes 1, 2, 4, and 3

51 Simplify the expression.

$$3\tfrac{2}{3} + 1\tfrac{1}{2} - 0.875 + 2^3(5 - 6)$$

    Ⓐ   9.17

    Ⓑ   3.63

    Ⓒ   -3.71

    Ⓓ   -4.13

52 Geneva has been assigned a project for her math class. She must pick 4 different sizes of a product and choose which size is the best buy. Her data is shown in the chart below.

Ray's Potato Chips

Package Size	Price
2-ounce bag	$0.69
8-ounce bag	$2.79
16-ounce bag	$5.12
40-ounce bag	$13.20

How should Geneva compare the package sizes and decide which size would be the best bargain? On the back of this page, explain your decision.

③ Practice Math Test

Part A

Directions: Find the correct answer.

1 The graph represents the number of bottles of water sold at a park each day and the high temperature for that day.

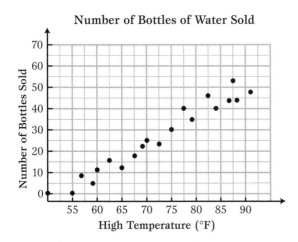

Number of Bottles of Water Sold

Based on the trend shown in the scatter plot, which choice is the best estimate for the number of bottles of water sold on a day when the high temperature is 80°F?

Ⓐ 30
Ⓑ 40
Ⓒ 65
Ⓓ 90

2 Arrange the given values in order from least to greatest.

19   -203   -3   1   -6 $\sqrt{36}$

Ⓕ -3, 1, -6, 19, $\sqrt{36}$, -203
Ⓖ $\sqrt{36}$, 19, 1, -3, -6, -203
Ⓗ -203, -6, -3, 1, $\sqrt{36}$, 19
Ⓙ -203, -6, -3, 1, 19, $\sqrt{36}$

3 How far will the wheel travel in 1 rotation? The diameter of the wheel is 19 inches. Approximate your answer to the nearest foot.

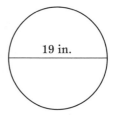

19 in.

Ⓐ 24 feet
Ⓑ 19 feet
Ⓒ 8 feet
Ⓓ 5 feet

4 McGuire High School plans to install a vending machine so students can buy snacks. The principal wants to find out what kinds of snacks students would like to be able to buy. Which process is a good way for the principal to collect this information?

Ⓕ Ask the parents during an open house.

Ⓖ Using an alphabetical list of the students attending the school, survey every tenth student.

Ⓗ Put a box in the office and let students vote as many times as they want to.

Ⓙ Survey about 30 of the boys attending the school.

GO ON ➡

5 The volume of the smaller cube is 8 cubic centimeters. What is the volume of the larger cube?

 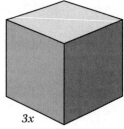

x

$3x$

Figures not drawn to scale.

    Ⓐ 142 cm^3

    Ⓑ 127 cm^3

    Ⓒ 172 cm^3

    Ⓓ 216 cm^3

6 To find the volume of the cone, which formula should be used?

    Ⓕ $l \times y \times h$

    Ⓖ πy^2

    Ⓗ $\pi y^2 \cdot h$

    Ⓙ $\frac{1}{3}\pi y^2 \cdot h$

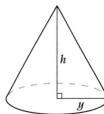

h

y

7 Which expression does NOT result in a number greater than **27**?

    Ⓐ $27 + 2 + |\text{-}2|$

    Ⓑ $27 \div \frac{1}{2} + |\text{-}2|$

    Ⓒ $27 \times \frac{1}{2} + |\text{-}2|$

    Ⓓ $27 + \frac{1}{2} + |\text{-}2|$

8 Rectangle *ABCD* was changed to form rectangle *WXYZ*.

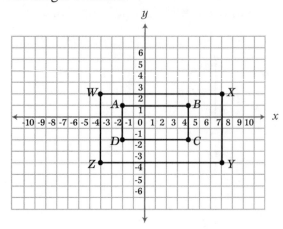

Select the scale factor used to change rectangle *ABCD* into rectangle *WXYZ*.

    Ⓕ $\frac{1}{3}$

    Ⓖ 2

    Ⓗ $\frac{1}{2}$

    Ⓙ 3

9 In the circle below, angle *A* is 55°. What is the measure of angle *B*?

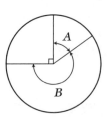

    Ⓐ 215°

    Ⓑ 220°

    Ⓒ 225°

    Ⓓ 295°

GO ON

Practice Math Test 3 (continued)

10 A graphic designer is creating the shape shown below. If $\overline{AB}$ is parallel to $\overline{CD}$ and $\overline{BC}$ is parallel to $\overline{AD}$, what is the measure of angle 4?

Ⓕ 60°
Ⓖ 70°
Ⓗ 80°
Ⓙ 85°

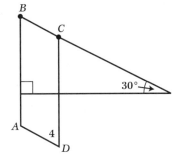

11 Which statement is FALSE?

Ⓐ If you multiply 20 by a number greater than 1, the answer will be greater than 20.

Ⓑ If you divide 20 by a number greater than 1, the answer will be less than 20.

Ⓒ If you multiply 20 by $\frac{1}{2}$ or $\frac{1}{5}$, the answer will be greater than 20.

Ⓓ If you divide 20 by $\frac{1}{2}$ or $\frac{1}{5}$, the answer will be greater than 20.

12 Which choice lists the given numbers from least to greatest?

$-\frac{8}{9}$ **-81%**   **-0.805**   **$-82\frac{1}{2}\%$**

Ⓕ $-82\frac{1}{2}\%$ -81% -0.805 $-\frac{8}{9}$

Ⓖ $-\frac{8}{9}$ $-82\frac{1}{2}\%$ -81% -0.805

Ⓗ -0.805 $-82\frac{1}{2}\%$ -81% $-\frac{8}{9}$

Ⓙ -81% -0.805 $-82\frac{1}{2}\%$ $-\frac{8}{9}$

13 Which coordinate graph displays the line for the points listed in the table?

x	y
-2	2
0	1
2	0
4	-1

Ⓐ 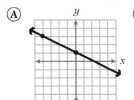   Ⓑ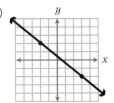

Ⓒ 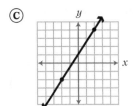   Ⓓ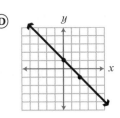

14 The manufacturer of a mouthwash has decided to increase the size of the bottle to hold 25% more mouthwash. If the original bottle held 20 ounces, how many ounces will the new bottle hold?

Ⓕ 5 ounces
Ⓖ 22.5 ounces
Ⓗ 25 ounces
Ⓙ 30 ounces

GO ON

15 A manufacturer makes 2 different sizes of soup cans. Approximately how much more volume does the larger can hold than the smaller can? Use: $V = \pi r^2 h$

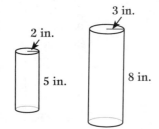

Ⓐ 163 in.^{3}

Ⓑ 101 in.^{3}

Ⓒ 88 in.^{3}

Ⓓ 44 in.^{3}

16

x	2	4	8
$2(x-3)$	-2	2	?

Which value is missing in the table?

Ⓕ 4

Ⓖ 6

Ⓗ 8

Ⓙ 10

17 Look at the expressions. Which value does NOT equal **20**?

Ⓐ $|20|$

Ⓑ $|-20|$

Ⓒ $4^2 - 2^2$

Ⓓ $5^2 - 5$

18 Which answer best represents the area and perimeter of the rectangle shown?

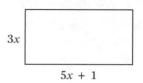

Ⓕ area = $15x^2 + 3x^2$
   perimeter = $8x + 2$

Ⓖ area = $15x^2 + 3x$
   perimeter = $16x + 2$

Ⓗ area = $15x^2 + 1$
   perimeter = $16x + 1$

Ⓙ area = $15x^2 + 1$
   perimeter = $8x - 1$

19 Javier wants to build a fence around a triangular-shaped garden. Using the dimensions provided below, how much fencing will he need to purchase?

Ⓐ 46 feet

Ⓑ 32 feet

Ⓒ 24 feet

Ⓓ 16 feet

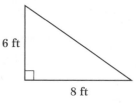

20 Which choice shows 2 values equivalent to **25%**?

Ⓕ 0.25 and $\frac{4}{16}$

Ⓖ 2.5 and $\frac{4}{16}$

Ⓗ 0.25 and $\frac{2}{5}$

Ⓙ 0.025 and $\frac{2}{5}$

GO ON

Practice Math Test 3 (continued)

21 The eighth-grade class sponsored a walkathon to raise money for cancer research. The 58 students raised $1,500 in the first 12 hours. Based on this rate, which proportion can be used to determine the amount (n) the students can expect to raise over the entire 36 hours of the walkathon?

- (A) $\frac{58}{12} = \frac{\$1,500}{n}$
- (B) $\frac{36}{12} = \frac{\$1,500}{n}$
- (C) $\frac{\$1,500}{58} = \frac{n}{36}$
- (D) $\frac{12}{\$1,500} = \frac{36}{n}$

22 Maria has 2 skirts—1 black and 1 gray. She has 3 blouses—1 pink, 1 striped, and 1 floral. She chooses a skirt and a blouse as an outfit. What is the probability that her outfit will include the pink blouse?

- (F) $\frac{1}{2}$
- (G) $\frac{1}{3}$
- (H) $\frac{5}{6}$
- (J) $\frac{1}{6}$

23 Which statement below correctly shows 0.000063 written in scientific notation?

- (A) $0.000063 = 6.3 \times 10^{6}$
- (B) $0.000063 = 6.3 \times 10^{-5}$
- (C) $0.000063 = 6.3 \times 10^{-7}$
- (D) $0.000063 = 6.3 \times 10^{-6}$

24 Candice drew a triangle without looking at the triangle that Andy drew. Under which condition would the triangles be congruent?

- (F) All angles are equal.
- (G) All sides are equal.
- (H) Both figures are right triangles.
- (J) Both triangles have the same perimeter.

25 At sunset, the temperature was 2°F below zero. By 12:00 noon the next day, the temperature had risen 27°. Which expression can be used to determine the temperature at noon?

- (A) -2 – 27
- (B) -2 + 27
- (C) 2 – 27
- (D) 2 + 27

26 What is the measure of angle Y?

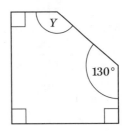

- (F) 360°
- (G) 190°
- (H) 140°
- (J) 130°

for Part A

27 If Figure M is rotated and then reflected, which diagram is correct?

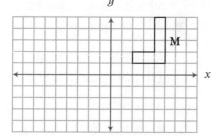

Ⓐ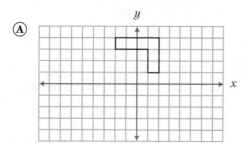

Ⓑ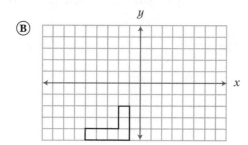

Ⓒ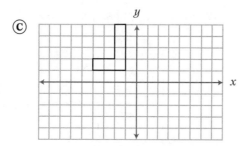

Ⓓ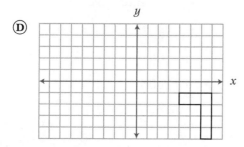

28 Whitney invested $200 in an account that earned 6% annual interest. She also invested $100 at 5.5% annual interest. How much interest did she earn at the end of the first year?

Ⓕ $11.50

Ⓖ $30.00

Ⓗ $17.50

Ⓙ $125.50

29 Using $x = -2$, solve: $2x - (3x + 4)$.

Ⓐ -14

Ⓑ -6

Ⓒ -2

Ⓓ 6

30 Which expression is equivalent to **29**?

Ⓕ $2^3 + 21$

Ⓖ $2^2 + 3^2 + \sqrt{25} + 14$

Ⓗ $\sqrt{81} + \sqrt{100} - 30$

Ⓙ $52 + \sqrt{16}$

31 Tawana tosses a fair 6-sided number cube 24 times. Predict how many of the 24 tosses will result in a number less than 3.

Ⓐ 2

Ⓑ 6

Ⓒ 8

Ⓓ 10

GO ON

32 Orlando had taken 5 tests in his history class and received the following test scores: **93**, **99**, **89**, **94**, and **91**. On his sixth test he scored a **60**. Choose the answer that will change the most as a result of the sixth test.

   Ⓕ the mean

   Ⓖ the maximum value

   Ⓗ the median

   Ⓙ the mode

33 Roberto tossed a fair coin 4 times, and heads was shown each time. What is the probability of heads being the outcome of his next toss?

   Ⓐ 1

   Ⓑ $\frac{4}{5}$

   Ⓒ $\frac{1}{2}$

   Ⓓ $\frac{1}{5}$

34 Victoria wants to paint the walls and ceiling of her bedroom but not the floor. How many gallons of paint are needed if a gallon of paint covers 400 square feet? Use the diagram to answer the question.

   Ⓕ 3 gallons

   Ⓖ $2\frac{1}{2}$ gallons

   Ⓗ 2 gallons

   Ⓙ $1\frac{1}{2}$ gallons

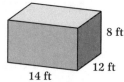

8 ft, 12 ft, 14 ft

35 A recipe for chocolate requires a 5:4 ratio of cocoa beans to milk. How many gallons of milk must be purchased if the company has 80 pounds of cocoa beans?

   Ⓐ 9 gallons

   Ⓑ 64 gallons

   Ⓒ 100 gallons

   Ⓓ 320 gallons

36 A package has been cut and laid flat.

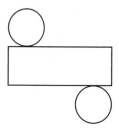

What was the three-dimensional shape of the package?

   Ⓕ cone

   Ⓖ cube

   Ⓗ cylinder

   Ⓙ pyramid

37 Simplify: $\frac{1}{2} + 6 \cdot 0.5 - 2 - (\frac{1}{2})^2$

   Ⓐ $-8\frac{1}{2}$

   Ⓑ $-1\frac{1}{2}$

   Ⓒ 1.25

   Ⓓ 8.5

GO ON

38 Solve this system of equations:

$$y = x - 1$$
$$x + y = 3$$

Ⓕ $x = 0, y = 3$

Ⓖ $x = 4, y = 3$

Ⓗ $x = -1, y = 4$

Ⓙ $x = 2, y = 1$

39 If $\triangle ABC$ is congruent to $\triangle DEF$, what is the measure of $\angle F$?

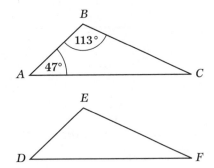

Ⓐ 20°

Ⓑ 47°

Ⓒ 67°

Ⓓ 30°

40 Which expression does NOT simplify to **$3x + 8$**?

Ⓕ $2(2x + 3) - 3(x + 2)$

Ⓖ $x + 2(x + 4)$

Ⓗ $5(x - 1) - 2x + 13$

Ⓙ $-2(2x - 1) + 7(x + 1) - 1$

41 Which statement is NOT true for the number **36**?

Ⓐ A multiple of 36 is 72.

Ⓑ The prime factors are 1 and 3.

Ⓒ The square root is 6.

Ⓓ The factors are 1, 2, 3, 4, 6, 9, 12, 18, 36.

42 Find the missing angle for the figure.

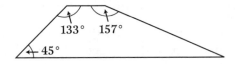

Ⓕ 133°

Ⓖ 82°

Ⓗ 45°

Ⓙ 25°

43 $\triangle ABC$ is similar to $\triangle DEF$. Find the measure of side $\overline{DF}$.

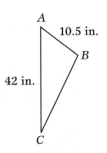 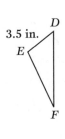

Ⓐ 7 inches

Ⓑ 14 inches

Ⓒ 21 inches

Ⓓ 26.25 inches

GO ON

44 The table below shows the number of students at Fairmount Middle School who prefer different types of music.

Rap	Rock	Jazz	Alternative
180	250	105	120

Which type of graph would best represent this data?

- Ⓕ stem-and-leaf plot
- Ⓖ scatter plot
- Ⓗ box-and-whisker plot
- Ⓙ bar graph

45 Nina measured some candy on a scale, which registered the following weight in ounces:

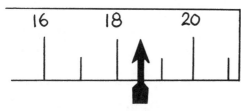

She wants to divide the candy into 5 equal bags. How much will each bag hold?

- Ⓐ 95 ounces
- Ⓑ 90 ounces
- Ⓒ 3.8 ounces
- Ⓓ 3.7 ounces

46 The cost of a long-distance phone call can be determined by the equation $C = 0.35m$ (C = total cost and m = number of minutes talked). Choose the table that contains values that used the equation.

Ⓕ
m	1	2	3	4
C	$0.35	$1.35	$1.75	$2.05

Ⓖ
m	1	2	3	4
C	$0.35	$1.35	$2.35	$4.35

Ⓗ
m	1	2	3	4
C	$0.30	$0.60	$0.90	$1.35

Ⓙ
m	1	2	3	4
C	$0.35	$0.70	$1.05	$1.40

47 An empty truck being used at a construction site weighs $2\frac{1}{4}$ tons. A worker loads the truck with $1\frac{2}{3}$ tons of gravel and $\frac{1}{2}$ ton of sand. How many tons does the loaded truck weigh?

- Ⓐ $4\frac{1}{2}$ tons
- Ⓑ $4\frac{2}{3}$ tons
- Ⓒ $4\frac{5}{12}$ tons
- Ⓓ 5 tons

GO ON

48 The city plans to install a fence that will divide a rectangular park into 2 sections—a picnic area and a playground. Using the dimensions below, how long should the fence be?

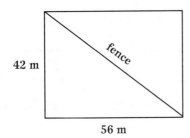

- Ⓕ 49 meters
- Ⓖ 70 meters
- Ⓗ 196 meters
- Ⓙ 4,900 meters

49 Which number line represents the solution for the inequality?

$$-1 \leq x + 2$$

Ⓐ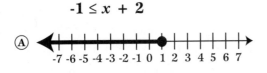

Ⓑ

Ⓒ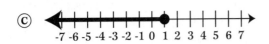

Ⓓ

50 A CD player costs $180.00. It is on sale for 20% off. The sales tax is 6.5%. How much does the CD player cost after the discount, including tax?

- Ⓕ $142.50
- Ⓖ $153.36
- Ⓗ $186.50
- Ⓙ $237.60

51 The mayor of a city is running for reelection this November. Three different preliminary opinion polls have been conducted prior to the election to show the proportion of voters who are expected to vote for the mayor. Each poll shows different results.

Poll 1: The percentage of voters expected to vote for the mayor is 54%.

Poll 2: Thirteen out of every 25 voters are expected to vote for the mayor.

Poll 3: There are 150,000 people who are expected to vote, and 59,000 of them are expected to vote to reelect the mayor.

Determine which of these polls shows the greatest favorable result for the mayor's reelection. On the back of this page, explain your decision.

Practice Math Test

Directions: Find the correct answer.

1 Ben brought a box of colored pencils to class. It contained 3 red, 2 blue, 4 green, 1 black, 2 yellow, and 3 orange pencils. If Ben randomly picks a pencil, what is the chance that he will choose a blue or an orange pencil?

Ⓐ $\frac{2}{15}$

Ⓑ $\frac{1}{5}$

Ⓒ $\frac{5}{14}$

Ⓓ $\frac{1}{3}$

2 If the measurements of this trapezoid were doubled, how would the change in size affect its perimeter and area?

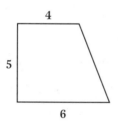

Ⓕ Both the perimeter and area would double in size.

Ⓖ The perimeter would double in size. The area would increase by 4 times.

Ⓗ The perimeter would double in size. The area would remain the same.

Ⓙ The area would double in size. The perimeter would increase by 3 times.

3 Tomas and his roommates Pirro and Tyler are renting a car for their 8-day vacation. Tyler can only go for 3 days so he only pays $\frac{3}{8}$ of the cost for rental. Pirro will only be there for 40% of the time so he wants to pay for 40% of the cost. If the total car rental is $128, how much will Tomas pay?

Ⓐ $28.80

Ⓑ $42.68

Ⓒ $48.32

Ⓓ $51.20

4 List the given numbers in order from greatest to least in value.

-12   0 |-15| -3 |-5| -7   1

Ⓕ |-15|, |-5|, 1, 0, -3, -7, -12

Ⓖ 0, 1, -3, |-5|, -7, -12, |-15|

Ⓗ |-15|, -12, -7, -3, 0, 1, |-5|

Ⓙ -12, -7, 0, 1, -3, |-5|, |-15|

5 Nick is buying a home-theater system that costs $895.00. He borrows the money from a bank that charges 3.5% interest annually. If he pays back the loan in 2 years, what is the total amount he will pay the bank?

Ⓐ $1,208.25

Ⓑ $958.75

Ⓒ $926.33

Ⓓ $902.00

GO ON ➡

6 Simplify the expression below.

$$\frac{1}{4}(8 \cdot 4 - 12 \div 3)$$

Ⓕ 7

Ⓖ $\frac{20}{12}$

Ⓗ -7

Ⓙ $-\frac{64}{12}$

7 What is the relationship between $\triangle ABC$ and $\triangle PRQ$?

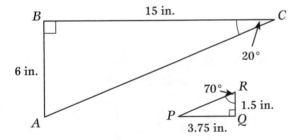

Ⓐ The triangles are congruent.

Ⓑ The triangles are equilateral.

Ⓒ The triangles are isosceles.

Ⓓ The triangles are similar.

8 When traveling in Canada, Lakeisha noticed a sign that read "Toronto 125 km." About how far was she from Toronto in miles (m)?

Use: $m = km \cdot 0.621$.

Ⓕ 250 miles

Ⓖ 125 miles

Ⓗ 80 miles

Ⓙ 41.5 miles

9 Which expression below has the greatest value?

Ⓐ 2

Ⓑ $|-12|$

Ⓒ $|4|$

Ⓓ $|-\sqrt{81}|$

10 The greatest distance from Mars to the Sun is 2.279×10^8 kilometers. What would this distance be in standard form?

Ⓕ 227,900,000 kilometers

Ⓖ 22,790,000 kilometers

Ⓗ 0.00000002279 kilometers

Ⓙ 2,279,000 kilometers

11 Solve the equation for the variable.

$$4(n - 4) = 6(n + 2)$$

Ⓐ $n = 3$

Ⓑ $n = -14$

Ⓒ $n = -3$

Ⓓ $n = 12$

12 Which expression is a *binomial*?

Ⓕ $\frac{1}{3}n$

Ⓖ $326r$

Ⓗ $0.4n^2$

Ⓙ $x + 1$

GO ON

13

Sam's Deli

Ham $4.00/lb

Turkey $3.50/lb

Beef $4.50/lb

Dill pickles.........$0.50 each

Bob's mom gave him $10.00 to purchase sandwich meat at the deli. He buys $\frac{3}{4}$ pound of ham, $\frac{1}{2}$ pound of beef, and $\frac{2}{3}$ pound of turkey. How many pickles will Bob be able to purchase with the change?

Ⓐ 2 dill pickles

Ⓑ 3 dill pickles

Ⓒ 4 dill pickles

Ⓓ 5 dill pickles

14 Which formula would be used to find the volume of this object?

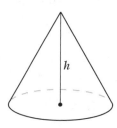

Ⓕ $V = l \cdot w \cdot h$

Ⓖ $V = \frac{1}{2}(b_1 + b_2) \cdot h$

Ⓗ $V = \frac{4}{3}\pi r^3$

Ⓙ $V = \frac{1}{3}\pi r^2 h$

15 Solve the equation for r.

$$-2(-4 \cdot 6) \div (-9 \div 3) = r$$

Ⓐ $r = 16$

Ⓑ $r = -8$

Ⓒ $r = 8$

Ⓓ $r = -16$

16 Which answer shows $\frac{5}{8}$ written as a percentage?

Ⓕ 0.625%

Ⓖ 1.6%

Ⓗ 62.5%

Ⓙ 160%

17 The volume of a sphere is found using the formula $V = \frac{4}{3}\pi r^3$. If the radius of the sphere is 2 feet, what is the volume of this hemisphere?

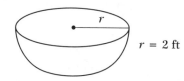

Ⓐ $\frac{24\pi}{3}$

Ⓑ $\frac{32\pi}{3}$

Ⓒ $\frac{16}{3}\pi$

Ⓓ 8π

GO ON

18 Which answer shows the given numbers in order from least to greatest?

$$\frac{3}{4} \qquad 0.623 \qquad 14\% \qquad |-6.2|$$

Ⓕ $\frac{3}{4}$ 0.623 |-6.2| 14%

Ⓖ |-6.2| 14%   0.623 $\frac{3}{4}$

Ⓗ 14%   0.623 $\frac{3}{4}$ |-6.2|

Ⓙ 0.623 |-6.2| 14% $\frac{3}{4}$

19 Solve the equation for x.

$$\frac{4x + 3}{x} = 5$$

Ⓐ $x = 4$

Ⓑ $x = 3$

Ⓒ $x = 2.5$

Ⓓ $x = -2$

20 What is the measure of $\angle B$?

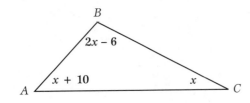

Ⓕ 44°

Ⓖ 47°

Ⓗ 82°

Ⓙ 180°

21 Identify the x-intercept and the y-intercept of the line on the graph.

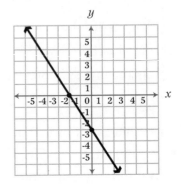

Ⓐ x-intercept (-3, 0)
   y-intercept (0, -2)

Ⓑ x-intercept (-2, 0)
   y-intercept (0, -3)

Ⓒ x-intercept (0, -2)
   y-intercept (-3, 0)

Ⓓ x-intercept (2, 0)
   y-intercept (-3, 0)

22 Which choice shows the statement below written in algebraic form?

The sum of ten times a number and sixteen is greater than four times the quotient of a number and five.

Ⓕ $10(n + 16) > 4n - 5$

Ⓖ $10(n + 16) \le 4\left(\frac{n}{5}\right)$

Ⓗ $10n + 16 = 4(n - 5)$

Ⓙ $10n + 16 > 4\left(\frac{n}{5}\right)$

GO ON

Practice Math Test 4 (continued)

23 If the value of x is doubled in the equation $x^2 = y$, what happens to the value of y?

ⓐ It gets doubled.

ⓑ It gets halved.

ⓒ It increases by a factor of 4.

ⓓ It increases by a factor of 5.

24 The expression $3x - 4$ is the simplified version of which expression below?

ⓕ $4(x - 2) - (x - 4)$

ⓖ $6(x + 1) - 3(x + 1)$

ⓗ $-5(x + 2) + 8(x + 1)$

ⓙ $5(x + 3) - 2(x + 5)$

25 The number line shows the solution to which inequality?

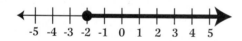

ⓐ $6x + 8 > -4$

ⓑ $2x - 6 \leq -10$

ⓒ $4x + 3 < -2$

ⓓ $3x + 4 \geq -2$

26 A deciliter is _____ kiloliters.

ⓕ 1,000

ⓖ 0.00001

ⓗ 0.0001

ⓙ 0.001

27 Which equation could be used to find the measure of side a of the triangle?

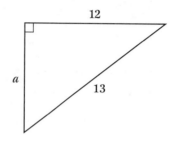

ⓐ $12 + 13 = a$

ⓑ $12^2 + a^2 = 13^2$

ⓒ $12^2 + 13^2 = a^2$

ⓓ $12^2 + a^2 = 13^2$

28 The building casts a shadow of 32 feet. Using proportions, find the length of the shadow (x) cast by the tree.

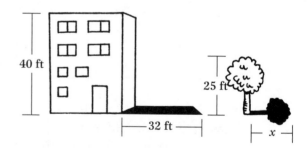

ⓕ 20 feet

ⓖ 18 feet

ⓗ 15 feet

ⓙ 12.5 feet

STOP

for Part A

29 Find the mean, median, and mode for the following set of data.

8, 12, 10, 7, 9, 4, 5, 7, 10, 7, 9

Ⓐ mean 12, median 9, mode 4

Ⓑ mean 8, median 4, mode 7

Ⓒ mean 8, median 8, mode 7

Ⓓ mean 8, median 9, mode 9

30 Which graph shows a slope of $-\frac{1}{2}$?

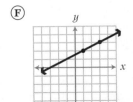 Ⓕ
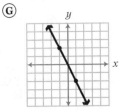 Ⓖ
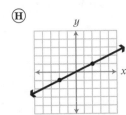 Ⓗ
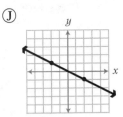 Ⓙ

31 Every 3 days Toni gives her little sister, Natasha, a shiny gold star. Every 4 days Natasha receives a blue star, and every 6 days she earns a red star. If Toni gives Natasha her first gold star on Wednesday, on which day will Natasha receive all 3 stars?

Ⓐ Thursday

Ⓑ Friday

Ⓒ Saturday

Ⓓ Sunday

32 A fair number cube is rolled 60 times and for 12 of the rolls it showed the number 4. If the same number cube is rolled 200 times, about how many times would you expect a 4 to be the result?

Ⓕ 20

Ⓖ 30

Ⓗ 40

Ⓙ 60

33 If M is a prime number, which statement is always TRUE?

Ⓐ $M + 1$ will never be a prime number.

Ⓑ $M + 2$ is an odd number.

Ⓒ $M + M$ is never a prime number.

Ⓓ $M + 1$ is an even number.

34 $\triangle ABC$ is similar to $\triangle DEF$. What is the length of $\overline{ED}$?

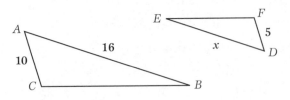

Ⓕ 8

Ⓖ 10

Ⓗ 11

Ⓙ 12

35 What is the surface area of this prism?

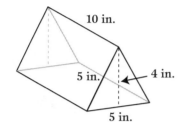

- Ⓐ 190 in.²
- Ⓑ 170 in.²
- Ⓒ 120 in.²
- Ⓓ 1,000 in.²

36 The bar graph shows the favorite summer activities of 600 eighth grade students. Based on the graph, which statement is TRUE?

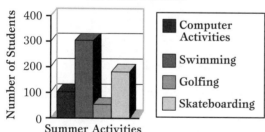

- Ⓕ About 25 % of the students like computer activities best.
- Ⓖ Only 10 % of the students enjoy playing golf.
- Ⓗ Skateboarding was the choice of 25 % of the students.
- Ⓙ More boys than girls like to swim.

37 Susan works at Pizza Palace. To get there from home, she can either walk the length and width of the block or cut across the field next to the business. About how much shorter is her walk if she cuts across the field?

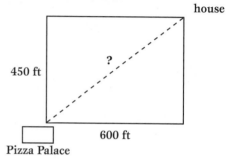

- Ⓐ 600 feet
- Ⓑ 500 feet
- Ⓒ 450 feet
- Ⓓ 300 feet

38 Look at the diagram. Hal has to paint the shape on the playground. How much area will this figure cover? Use π = **3.14**.

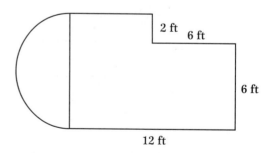

- Ⓕ 97.12 ft²
- Ⓖ 109.12 ft²
- Ⓗ 121.12 ft²
- Ⓙ 156.42 ft²

39 Which list contains only three-dimensional objects?

    Ⓐ pentagon, sphere, octahedron

    Ⓑ pyramid, quadrilateral, cone

    Ⓒ prism, circle, polygon

    Ⓓ sphere, cone, prism

40 Solve the equation: $2\frac{1}{3} \div \frac{5}{6} = x$

    Ⓕ $x = 2\frac{5}{18}$

    Ⓖ $x = 2\frac{4}{5}$

    Ⓗ $x = \frac{7}{6}$

    Ⓙ $x = \frac{4}{5}$

41 Lines $\overline{AB}$ and $\overline{RM}$ are perpendicular to each other. Line $\overline{CD}$ is parallel to line $\overline{RM}$. If $\angle AOE$ is 43.5°, what is the measure of $\angle 2$?

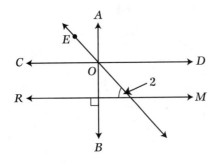

    Ⓐ 43.5°

    Ⓑ 46.5°

    Ⓒ 50.5°

    Ⓓ 90°

42 Which point is NOT on $\overleftrightarrow{AB}$?

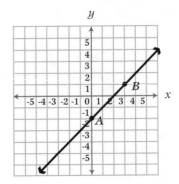

    Ⓕ point (3, 1)

    Ⓖ point (0, -2)

    Ⓗ point (2, 0)

    Ⓙ point (1, 3)

43 Which equation has the given solution?

$$x \le 12$$

    Ⓐ $3x + 3 \ge 12$

    Ⓑ $6x \ge 2x + 8$

    Ⓒ $4x - 12 \le 3x$

    Ⓓ $\frac{1}{2}x + 6 \ge 24x$

44 Which choice has the greatest value?

    Ⓕ 4^2

    Ⓖ $(-3)^2$

    Ⓗ $-\sqrt{49}$

    Ⓙ $\sqrt{144}$

GO ON

45 Mitch drove 358 miles to Memphis, Tennessee, and his average speed was 55 miles per hour. If he left his house at 10:00 A.M. and made only 1 stop for a 30-minute lunch break, about what time did he arrive?

Ⓐ 3:00 P.M.

Ⓑ 4:00 P.M.

Ⓒ 5:00 P.M.

Ⓓ 6:00 P.M.

46 Out of 200 people surveyed, the following data was gathered about favorite flavors of ice cream.

50 prefer vanilla
60 prefer strawberry
70 prefer chocolate
10 don't like ice cream
10 prefer sherbet

Which graph best represents the data?

Ⓕ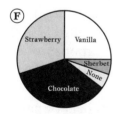

Ⓖ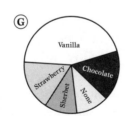

Ⓗ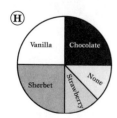

Ⓙ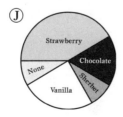

47 Look at the diagram of the box. If all of the dimensions were doubled, what would you expect to happen to the box's volume?

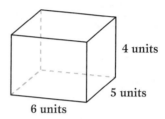

Ⓐ The volume should double in size.

Ⓑ The volume will increase by a factor of 3.

Ⓒ The volume will increase by a factor of 8.

Ⓓ You cannot predict what will happen.

48 If $\triangle RST \cong \triangle ABC$, what is the measure of $\angle T$?

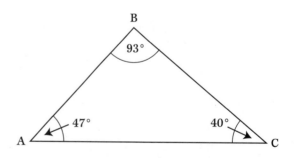

Ⓕ 180°

Ⓖ 93°

Ⓗ 47°

Ⓙ 40°

GO ON

Practice Math Test 4 (continued)

49 Look at each graph by itself. If △*FGH* is reflected across the *y*-axis, which figure would result?

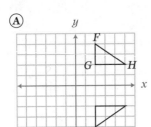 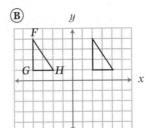 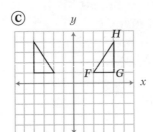 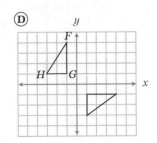

50 Which triangles are proportional?

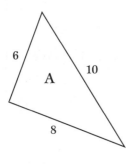  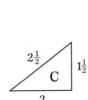

Ⓕ Triangles A and C

Ⓖ Triangles B and C

Ⓗ Triangles C and D

Ⓙ Triangles A and B

51

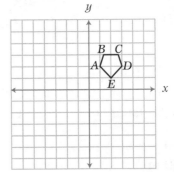

Move figure *ABCD* from its original position in Quadrant I to a new position in Quadrant III. Explain 2 different methods in which this could be accomplished and draw the new position of the figure. Use the following transformations: rotation, reflection, and translation. Write your explanation on the back of this page or on another sheet of paper.

STOP

Answer Sheet

STUDENT'S NAME			SCHOOL
LAST	FIRST	MI	TEACHER

GRADE ③ ④ ⑤ ⑥ ⑦ ⑧

FEMALE ○   MALE ○

BIRTH DATE

MONTH	DAY	YEAR

JAN ○   ⓪ ⓪   ⓪ ⓪
FEB ○   ① ①   ① ①
MAR ○   ② ②   ② ②
APR ○   ③ ③   ③ ③
MAY ○   ④ ④
JUN ○   ⑤ ⑤
JUL ○   ⑥ ⑥
AUG ○   ⑦ ⑦
SEP ○   ⑧ ⑧
OCT ○   ⑨ ⑨
NOV ○
DEC ○

(Name grid bubbles: A B C D E F G H I J K L M N O P Q R S T U V W X Y Z)

Directions: Mark your answers carefully. Be sure to fill in each bubble completely.

1 Ⓐ Ⓑ Ⓒ Ⓓ	14 Ⓕ Ⓖ Ⓗ Ⓙ	27 Ⓐ Ⓑ Ⓒ Ⓓ	40 Ⓕ Ⓖ Ⓗ Ⓙ
2 Ⓕ Ⓖ Ⓗ Ⓙ	15 Ⓐ Ⓑ Ⓒ Ⓓ	28 Ⓕ Ⓖ Ⓗ Ⓙ	41 Ⓐ Ⓑ Ⓒ Ⓓ
3 Ⓐ Ⓑ Ⓒ Ⓓ	16 Ⓕ Ⓖ Ⓗ Ⓙ	29 Ⓐ Ⓑ Ⓒ Ⓓ	42 Ⓕ Ⓖ Ⓗ Ⓙ
4 Ⓕ Ⓖ Ⓗ Ⓙ	17 Ⓐ Ⓑ Ⓒ Ⓓ	30 Ⓕ Ⓖ Ⓗ Ⓙ	43 Ⓐ Ⓑ Ⓒ Ⓓ
5 Ⓐ Ⓑ Ⓒ Ⓓ	18 Ⓕ Ⓖ Ⓗ Ⓙ	31 Ⓐ Ⓑ Ⓒ Ⓓ	44 Ⓕ Ⓖ Ⓗ Ⓙ
6 Ⓕ Ⓖ Ⓗ Ⓙ	19 Ⓐ Ⓑ Ⓒ Ⓓ	32 Ⓕ Ⓖ Ⓗ Ⓙ	45 Ⓐ Ⓑ Ⓒ Ⓓ
7 Ⓐ Ⓑ Ⓒ Ⓓ	20 Ⓕ Ⓖ Ⓗ Ⓙ	33 Ⓐ Ⓑ Ⓒ Ⓓ	46 Ⓕ Ⓖ Ⓗ Ⓙ
8 Ⓕ Ⓖ Ⓗ Ⓙ	21 Ⓐ Ⓑ Ⓒ Ⓓ	34 Ⓕ Ⓖ Ⓗ Ⓙ	47 Ⓐ Ⓑ Ⓒ Ⓓ
9 Ⓐ Ⓑ Ⓒ Ⓓ	22 Ⓕ Ⓖ Ⓗ Ⓙ	35 Ⓐ Ⓑ Ⓒ Ⓓ	48 Ⓕ Ⓖ Ⓗ Ⓙ
10 Ⓕ Ⓖ Ⓗ Ⓙ	23 Ⓐ Ⓑ Ⓒ Ⓓ	36 Ⓕ Ⓖ Ⓗ Ⓙ	49 Ⓐ Ⓑ Ⓒ Ⓓ
11 Ⓐ Ⓑ Ⓒ Ⓓ	24 Ⓕ Ⓖ Ⓗ Ⓙ	37 Ⓐ Ⓑ Ⓒ Ⓓ	50 Ⓕ Ⓖ Ⓗ Ⓙ
12 Ⓕ Ⓖ Ⓗ Ⓙ	25 Ⓐ Ⓑ Ⓒ Ⓓ	38 Ⓕ Ⓖ Ⓗ Ⓙ	51 Ⓐ Ⓑ Ⓒ Ⓓ
13 Ⓐ Ⓑ Ⓒ Ⓓ	26 Ⓕ Ⓖ Ⓗ Ⓙ	39 Ⓐ Ⓑ Ⓒ Ⓓ	

Answer Key

Practice Math Test 1

1	C	26	H
2	H	27	A
3	D	28	J
4	H	29	B
5	B	30	H
6	J	31	B
7	C	32	G
8	J	33	A
9	B	34	J
10	G	35	A
11	B	36	F
12	J	37	D
13	D	38	J
14	H	39	A
15	D	40	H
16	F	41	C
17	B	42	H
18	F	43	B
19	C	44	F
20	J	45	B
21	C	46	F
22	F	47	C
23	C	48	G
24	G		
25	B		

Practice Math Test 2

1	B	27	D
2	J	28	G
3	A	29	C
4	J	30	H
5	C	31	C
6	G	32	F
7	D	33	D
8	F	34	G
9	B	35	C
10	F	36	J
11	D	37	B
12	J	38	H
13	D	39	B
14	J	40	H
15	A	41	D
16	G	42	G
17	D	43	C
18	H	44	G
19	B	45	C
20	H	46	H
21	D	47	A
22	G	48	J
23	C	49	C
24	F	50	G
25	D	51	C
26	G		

Practice Math Test 3

1	B	26	H
2	H	27	B
3	D	28	H
4	G	29	C
5	D	30	F
6	J	31	C
7	C	32	F
8	G	33	C
9	A	34	J
10	F	35	B
11	C	36	H
12	G	37	C
13	A	38	J
14	H	39	A
15	A	40	F
16	J	41	B
17	C	42	J
18	G	43	B
19	C	44	J
20	F	45	D
21	D	46	J
22	G	47	C
23	B	48	G
24	G	49	D
25	B	50	G

Practice Math Test 4

1	D	26	H
2	G	27	B
3	A	28	F
4	F	29	C
5	B	30	J
6	F	31	B
7	D	32	G
8	H	33	C
9	B	34	F
10	F	35	B
11	B	36	H
12	J	37	D
13	C	38	G
14	J	39	D
15	D	40	G
16	H	41	B
17	C	42	J
18	H	43	C
19	B	44	F
20	H	45	C
21	B	46	F
22	J	47	C
23	C	48	J
24	F	49	C
25	D	50	F

49 The answer should explain how all students had a chance to be selected. An example may be to put the names of all 7th graders in a hat and the names of all 8th graders in a second hat and then draw 30 names from each hat.

52 Geneva must figure the cost per unit (ounce) and compare the unit cost to find the best buy. The 16-ounce bag is the best buy.

51 Poll 1 shows the greatest favorable results for the mayor. To compare the results of the opinion polls, students can change the outcomes to percentages:
Poll 1—54%,
Poll 2—52%, and
Poll 3—about 39%.

51 Answers will vary. For example, figure *ABCD* could be rotated 180° around the origin and then translated 3 units down. For the second method, the shape could be reflected across the *x*-axis and the *y*-axis and finally translated 3 units down.